The 46 Adirondack High Peaks

Personal Journal Of:

_____

D1445385

Rank	Peak	Elevation	Page
1	Marcy	5344	4
2	Algonquin	5114	5
3	Haystack	4960	6
4	Skylight	4926	7
5	Whiteface	4867	8
6	Dix	4857	9
7	Gray	4840	10
8	Iroquois Peak	4840	11
9	Basin	4827	12
10	Gothics	4736	13
11	Colden	4714	14
12	Giant	4627	15
13	Nippletop	4620	16
14	Santanoni	4607	17
15	Redfield	4606	18
16	Wright Peak	4580	19
17	Saddleback	4515	20
18	Panther	4442	21
19	TableTop	4427	22
20	Rocky Peak	4420	23
21	Macomb	4405	24
22	Armstrong	4400	25
23	Hough	4400	26
24	Seward	4361	27
25	Marshall	4360	28
26	Allen	4340	29

27	Big Slide	4240	30
28	Esther	4240	31
29	Upper Wolf Jaw	4185	32
30	Lower Wolf Jaw	4175	33
31	Street	4166	34
32	Phelps	4161	35
33	Donaldson	4140	36
34	Seymour	4120	37
35	Sawteeth	4100	38
36	Cascade	4098	39
37	South Dix	4060	40
38	Porter	4059	41
39	Colvin	4057	42
40	Emmons	4040	43
41	Dial	4020	44
42	East Dix	4012	45
43	Blake Peak	3960	46
44	Cliff	3960	47
45	Nye	3895	48
46	Couchsachraga	3820	49
	MacNaughton*	4000	50

Elevation: 5,344

Peak Rank: 1

Date Hiked:

Hiked With:

Notes:

_____

_____

_____

_____

_____

_____

_____

_____

_____

_____

_____

_____

_____

_____

_____

_____

_____

_____

_____

_____

_____

_____

Algonquin

Elevation: 5,114

Peak Rank: 2

Date Hiked:

Hiked With:

Notes:

_____

_____

_____

_____

_____

_____

_____

_____

_____

_____

_____

_____

_____

_____

_____

_____

_____

_____

_____

_____

_____

Haystack

Elevation: 4,960

Peak Rank: 3

Date Hiked:

Hiked With:

Notes:

_____
_____
_____
_____
_____
_____
_____
_____
_____
_____
_____
_____
_____
_____
_____
_____
_____
_____
_____
_____
_____
_____

Skylight

Elevation: 4,926

Peak Rank: 4

Date Hiked:

Hiked With:

Notes:

_____
_____
_____
_____
_____
_____
_____
_____
_____
_____
_____
_____
_____
_____
_____
_____
_____
_____
_____
_____
_____
_____
_____

Whiteface

Elevation: 4,867

Peak Rank: 5

Date Hiked:

Hiked With:

Notes:

_____
_____
_____
_____
_____
_____
_____
_____
_____
_____
_____
_____
_____
_____
_____
_____
_____
_____
_____
_____
_____
_____

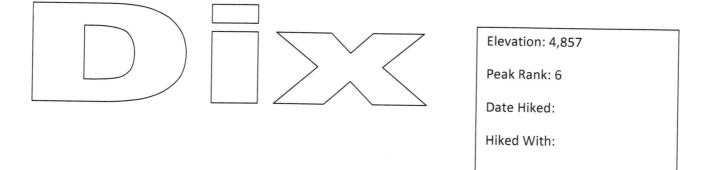

Elevation: 4,857

Peak Rank: 6

Date Hiked:

Hiked With:

Notes:

_____

_____

_____

_____

_____

_____

_____

_____

_____

_____

_____

_____

_____

_____

_____

_____

_____

_____

_____

_____

_____

_____

Elevation: 4,840

Peak Rank: 7

Date Hiked:

Hiked With:

Notes:

_____
_____
_____
_____
_____
_____
_____
_____
_____
_____
_____
_____
_____
_____
_____
_____
_____
_____
_____
_____
_____
_____

Iroquois Peak

Elevation: 4,840

Peak Rank: 8

Date Hiked:

Hiked With:

Notes:

Elevation: 4,827

Peak Rank: 9

Date Hiked:

Hiked With:

Notes:

_____

_____

_____

_____

_____

_____

_____

_____

_____

_____

_____

_____

_____

_____

_____

_____

_____

_____

_____

_____

_____

Gothics

Elevation: 4,736

Peak Rank: 10

Date Hiked:

Hiked With:

Notes:

_____

_____

_____

_____

_____

_____

_____

_____

_____

_____

_____

_____

_____

_____

_____

_____

_____

_____

_____

_____

_____

_____

_____

_____

Colden

Elevation: 4,714

Peak Rank: 11

Date Hiked:

Hiked With:

Notes:

_____

_____

_____

_____

_____

_____

_____

_____

_____

_____

_____

_____

_____

_____

_____

_____

_____

_____

_____

_____

_____

_____

Giant

Elevation: 4,627

Peak Rank: 12

Date Hiked:

Hiked With:

Notes:

_____

_____

_____

_____

_____

_____

_____

_____

_____

_____

_____

_____

_____

_____

_____

_____

_____

_____

_____

_____

Nippletop

Elevation: 4,620

Peak Rank: 13

Date Hiked:

Hiked With:

Notes:

_____

_____

_____

_____

_____

_____

_____

_____

_____

_____

_____

_____

_____

_____

_____

_____

_____

_____

_____

_____

Santanoni

Elevation: 4,607

Peak Rank: 14

Date Hiked:

Hiked With:

Notes:

_____

_____

_____

_____

_____

_____

_____

_____

_____

_____

_____

_____

_____

_____

_____

_____

_____

_____

_____

_____

_____

_____

Redfield

Elevation: 4,606

Peak Rank: 15

Date Hiked:

Hiked With:

Notes:

_____

_____

_____

_____

_____

_____

_____

_____

_____

_____

_____

_____

_____

_____

_____

_____

_____

_____

_____

_____

_____

_____

Wright Peak

Elevation: 4,580

Peak Rank: 16

Date Hiked:

Hiked With:

Notes:

_____
_____
_____
_____
_____
_____
_____
_____
_____
_____
_____
_____
_____
_____
_____
_____
_____
_____
_____
_____
_____
_____
_____
_____

Saddleback

Elevation: 4,515

Peak Rank: 17

Date Hiked:

Hiked With:

Notes:

_____
_____
_____
_____
_____
_____
_____
_____
_____
_____
_____
_____
_____
_____
_____
_____
_____
_____
_____
_____
_____
_____

Panther

Elevation: 4,442

Peak Rank: 18

Date Hiked:

Hiked With:

Notes:

_____

_____

_____

_____

_____

_____

_____

_____

_____

_____

_____

_____

_____

_____

_____

_____

_____

_____

_____

_____

_____

_____

_____

Tabletop

Elevation: 4,427

Peak Rank: 19

Date Hiked:

Hiked With:

Notes:

_____

_____

_____

_____

_____

_____

_____

_____

_____

_____

_____

_____

_____

_____

_____

_____

_____

_____

_____

_____

_____

_____

Rocky Peak

Elevation: 4,420

Peak Rank: 20

Date Hiked:

Hiked With:

Notes:

_____
_____
_____
_____
_____
_____
_____
_____
_____
_____
_____
_____
_____
_____
_____
_____
_____
_____
_____
_____
_____
_____
_____
_____

Macomb

Elevation: 4,405

Peak Rank: 21

Date Hiked:

Hiked With:

Notes:

_____
_____
_____
_____
_____
_____
_____
_____
_____
_____
_____
_____
_____
_____
_____
_____
_____
_____
_____
_____
_____
_____

Armstrong

Elevation: 4,400

Peak Rank: 22

Date Hiked:

Hiked With:

Notes:

_____
_____
_____
_____
_____
_____
_____
_____
_____
_____
_____
_____
_____
_____
_____
_____
_____
_____
_____
_____
_____
_____

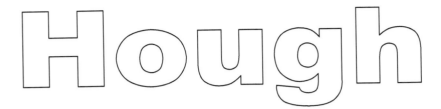

Elevation: 4,400

Peak Rank: 23

Date Hiked:

Hiked With:

Notes:

_____

_____

_____

_____

_____

_____

_____

_____

_____

_____

_____

_____

_____

_____

_____

_____

_____

_____

_____

_____

_____

_____

_____

Seward

Elevation: 4,361

Peak Rank: 24

Date Hiked:

Hiked With:

Notes:

_____
_____
_____
_____
_____
_____
_____
_____
_____
_____
_____
_____
_____
_____
_____
_____
_____
_____
_____
_____
_____
_____
_____
_____
_____

Marshall

Elevation: 4,360

Peak Rank: 25

Date Hiked:

Hiked With:

Notes:

_____

_____

_____

_____

_____

_____

_____

_____

_____

_____

_____

_____

_____

_____

_____

_____

_____

_____

_____

_____

_____

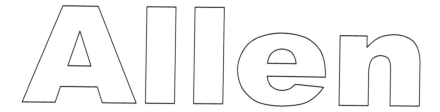

Elevation: 4,340

Peak Rank: 26

Date Hiked:

Hiked With:

Notes:

_____

_____

_____

_____

_____

_____

_____

_____

_____

_____

_____

_____

_____

_____

_____

_____

_____

_____

_____

_____

_____

_____

_____

Big Slide

Elevation: 4,240

Peak Rank: 27

Date Hiked:

Hiked With:

Notes:

_____
_____
_____
_____
_____
_____
_____
_____
_____
_____
_____
_____
_____
_____
_____
_____
_____
_____
_____
_____
_____
_____

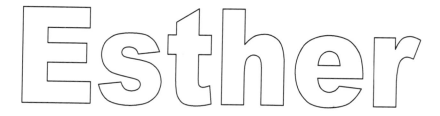

Elevation: 4,240

Peak Rank: 28

Date Hiked:

Hiked With:

Notes:

_____
_____
_____
_____
_____
_____
_____
_____
_____
_____
_____
_____
_____
_____
_____
_____
_____
_____
_____
_____

Upper Wolf Jaw

Elevation: 4,185

Peak Rank: 29

Date Hiked:

Hiked With:

Notes:

_____

_____

_____

_____

_____

_____

_____

_____

_____

_____

_____

_____

_____

_____

_____

_____

_____

_____

_____

_____

_____

_____

_____

Lower Wolf Jaw

Elevation: 4,175

Peak Rank: 30

Date Hiked:

Hiked With:

Notes:

_____
_____
_____
_____
_____
_____
_____
_____
_____
_____
_____
_____
_____
_____
_____
_____
_____
_____
_____
_____
_____
_____
_____
_____

Street

Elevation: 4,166

Peak Rank: 31

Date Hiked:

Hiked With:

Notes:

_____

_____

_____

_____

_____

_____

_____

_____

_____

_____

_____

_____

_____

_____

_____

_____

_____

_____

_____

_____

_____

_____

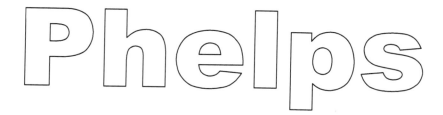

Elevation: 4,161

Peak Rank: 32

Date Hiked:

Hiked With:

Notes:

Donaldson

Elevation: 4,140

Peak Rank: 33

Date Hiked:

Hiked With:

Notes:

_____
_____
_____
_____
_____
_____
_____
_____
_____
_____
_____
_____
_____
_____
_____
_____
_____
_____
_____
_____
_____
_____

Seymour

Elevation: 4,120

Peak Rank: 34

Date Hiked:

Hiked With:

Notes:

_____
_____
_____
_____
_____
_____
_____
_____
_____
_____
_____
_____
_____
_____
_____
_____
_____
_____
_____
_____
_____
_____

Sawteeth

Elevation: 4,100

Peak Rank: 35

Date Hiked:

Hiked With:

Notes:

_____
_____
_____
_____
_____
_____
_____
_____
_____
_____
_____
_____
_____
_____
_____
_____
_____
_____
_____
_____
_____
_____

Cascade

Elevation: 4,098

Peak Rank: 36

Date Hiked:

Hiked With:

Notes:

_____
_____
_____
_____
_____
_____
_____
_____
_____
_____
_____
_____
_____
_____
_____
_____
_____
_____
_____
_____
_____
_____

South Dix

Elevation: 4,060

Peak Rank: 37

Date Hiked:

Hiked With:

Notes:

Elevation: 4,059

Peak Rank: 38

Date Hiked:

Hiked With:

Notes:

_____

_____

_____

_____

_____

_____

_____

_____

_____

_____

_____

_____

_____

_____

_____

_____

_____

_____

_____

_____

_____

_____

Colvin

Elevation: 4,057

Peak Rank: 39

Date Hiked:

Hiked With:

Notes:

Emmons

Elevation: 4,040

Peak Rank: 40

Date Hiked:

Hiked With:

Notes:

_____
_____
_____
_____
_____
_____
_____
_____
_____
_____
_____
_____
_____
_____
_____
_____
_____
_____
_____
_____
_____
_____

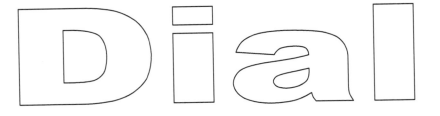

Elevation: 4,020

Peak Rank: 41

Date Hiked:

Hiked With:

Notes:

_____

_____

_____

_____

_____

_____

_____

_____

_____

_____

_____

_____

_____

_____

_____

_____

_____

_____

_____

_____

_____

_____

East Dix

Elevation: 4,012

Peak Rank: 42

Date Hiked:

Hiked With:

Notes:

_____
_____
_____
_____
_____
_____
_____
_____
_____
_____
_____
_____
_____
_____
_____
_____
_____
_____
_____
_____
_____
_____

Blake Peak

Elevation: 3,960

Peak Rank: 43

Date Hiked:

Hiked With:

Notes:

_____

_____

_____

_____

_____

_____

_____

_____

_____

_____

_____

_____

_____

_____

_____

_____

_____

_____

_____

_____

_____

_____

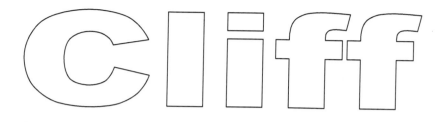

Elevation: 3,960

Peak Rank: 44

Date Hiked:

Hiked With:

Notes:

_____

_____

_____

_____

_____

_____

_____

_____

_____

_____

_____

_____

_____

_____

_____

_____

_____

_____

_____

_____

_____

_____

Elevation: 3,895

Peak Rank: 45

Date Hiked:

Hiked With:

Notes:

_____

_____

_____

_____

_____

_____

_____

_____

_____

_____

_____

_____

_____

_____

_____

_____

_____

_____

_____

_____

_____

_____

Couchsachraga

Elevation: 3,820

Peak Rank: 46

Date Hiked:

Hiked With:

Notes:

_____
_____
_____
_____
_____
_____
_____
_____
_____
_____
_____
_____
_____
_____
_____
_____
_____
_____
_____
_____
_____
_____

MacNoughton

Elevation: 4,000
Peak Rank: Not Ranked
Date Hiked:
Hiked With:

*Although MacNoughton is included in this journal, it is not a required climb. After the original 46 High Peaks were defined, a USGS study found MacNoughton to be 4,000 feet, the original cutoff to be considered a high peak.

Notes:

_____

_____

_____

_____

_____

_____

_____

_____

_____

_____

_____

_____

_____

_____

_____

_____

_____

_____

_____

_____

_____

_____

Made in the USA
Lexington, KY
08 June 2012